The Art of Apprenticeship

Azul Terronez

The Art of Apprenticeship

Blaze Publishing

DEDICATION

To Steve Vannoy, Skylar & Josiah Terronez,
Lori Gillespie and Joan Soria

This book was written because of the continued support of
my family—I dedicate this book to you. A special thanks to
all of those people who served as my teacher over the years—
your guidance has been invaluable.

Table of Contents

Acknowledgments .... *vii*

Introduction .... *ix*

Chapter 1: What Is Your Gift? *1*

Chapter 2: Creativity, Discovery and Passion *11*

Chapter 3: The Art of Failure *23*

Chapter 4: The Connection Revolution *33*

Chapter 5: Breaking Away from the Status Quo *41*

Chapter 6: Hack Your Learning *55*

Chapter 7: Pick Yourself *67*

Chapter 8: Finding Your Kick-Ass Mentor *75*

Chapter 9: Why an Apprenticeship? *85*

Chapter 10: Setting up Your Own Apprenticeship *91*

About The Author *101*

ACKNOWLEDGMENTS

I am so grateful for the opportunity to share my learning with the world. Writing this book has been a dream for me. I am grateful for the three Gurus: James Roper, Chandler Bolt and Tyler Wagner. I also want to thank the members of the Best Selling Book System—you all rock!

A special thanks to Pat Flynn and Chris Ducker and the members of The 1 Day Business Breakthrough mastermind group for inspiring me to make this book even larger than it was intended to be.

INTRODUCTION

Have you ever wondered what your life would be like if you could actually do what you love without having to go back to school to reinvent yourself? In The Art of Apprenticeship, international educational consultant and coach Azul Terronez cracks the code on how to uncover your passion and learn the ropes from successful mentors in any field.

For those tired of the grind who want to escape the 9-to-5—and anyone else who wants to leap from the status quo and do something new—The Art of Apprenticeship reveals an unconventional, fresh and simple pathway to break into any business, entrepreneurial venture or passion.

Learn how to put yourself out there, harness the power within yourself and the connection revolution to propel yourself forward to living the life you've always dreamed of but didn't have the courage or know-how to pursue.

Chapter 1

What Is Your Gift?

"The best way to find yourself is to lose yourself in the service of others."

—*Gandhi*

Our humanity, like our natural desire to discover, play and create, is also built around the nature of giving. It seems innate to love our children, our family, our significant other and our friends, but what doesn't seem natural is loving the larger world. I don't mean the world that requires world peace at all times, I mean loving the world known as humanity. We contribute to humanity positively or negatively depending on how conscience we are of the giving we do.

Giving to the world makes you a part of it. Holding on to our gift that was intended to be a part of the world leaves us depressed, feeling incomplete, unloved and unappreciated.

Gratitude comes from both giving and receiving. When someone accepts our gift we feel valued, appreciated and honored. One reason is that to be valued at our work or for our work is one of the top needs we have.

We need to feel appreciated to grow, flourish and be a giver. When we ignore our gifts we actually dwindle as humans. Have you ever noticed a young child that was so excited to share a drawing with a parent? Or a small craft or piece of art? My children love it when I appreciate and notice what they have created. They feel proud and joyful. The opposite is true if I ignore the self-proclaimed piece of art—they feel rejected, worthless, and eventually even begin to think that their gift doesn't matter; that perhaps if it were better it would be worth creating. As we grow older and the insecurities of judgment set in we convince ourselves that we aren't capable of creating work worth sharing, which is not true. Schools, in fact, help reinforce the idea that our work is constantly not good enough. Teachers return papers with red marks, coaches place us on second string and peers evaluate each others' value based on these perceived positions in the world.

The reason a parent cherishes a piece of work from a child is because they created it; because a parent sees the potential in the person and accepts the gift as a way of recognizing that fact. Your gift to the world is one of the major ways you contribute to the world, your community, your tribe, your family, yourself.

We must remember that our gift is not perfect work. Our gift only becomes a gift when we choose to give something of value away. If we don't give it, it's just an object, a thing, a piece of work. Giving is important because it says who I am is good enough . . . it's what I have to offer, not all I have to offer.

Your Gift to the World Creates a Life Worth Living, Not Just Mere Existence, But Honest Living.

Many people try to earn or buy the happiness that comes from sharing their gift. They get jobs that earn big money or start a business that's lucrative so that through the money they can be happy, but the work they are in isn't fulfilling, isn't their gift. So, they buy toys, cars, houses, take elaborate vacations, only to return to work that is empty and almost painful. They struggle to leave because they say to themselves or hear from others how good they are at what they do. They can't seem to turn down the opportunities and more money that seem to come, but the money doesn't fulfill them.

So they start a new job, get a promotion, change positions in the company and maybe even build a different business, earning even more money, which enables them to buy more toys and things to distract them from the things that they know they should be focusing on. None of these promotions nor changes seem to fill them, and so they start to feel like the relationship they are in isn't working; they notice other people and begin to think that their unhappiness comes from their partner or spouse. They decide that they need to move to new neighborhoods, cities, countries in search of their happiness but what they are missing is sharing their gift with the world.

Your gift is what creates abundance in your life. It's the thing that changes everything for you. It's the thing that the happiest people have found. In *The Alchemist*, Paulo says that the soul of the world longs to bring you the things that you long for. The soul of the world sends us messages and clues to help us but we often ignore those prompts. Your gift should bring you joy. Your gift should be something that you easily give away. You should feel almost compelled to do it, even if there were no money involved; it fills you, drives you, even wakes you at night or appears in your day dreams (if you still afford yourself this luxury).

I remember vividly being woken by something in the middle of the night that compelled me to write; to write down what I was learning. It didn't make sense—why would I or why should I write down what I am learning about myself? Who really cares besides me? What will I do with it? The more I listened to that voice the more I had to say, the more I wanted to tell people what I was discovering. The more I looked inside of who I was the more I found that my gift was to share the things I was learning with the world, not because it was perfect, but because I wanted to show what I was doing, who I was, and it felt great!

What is Your Gift and How Do You Know What It Is?

Your gift is what creates the foundation for meaningful work. But maybe you are saying, "Isn't a gift a talent?" But a gift is not just a talent though it can be something you are good at, maybe even the best at. In fact, you may have yet to discover it. Maybe you are 16 years old and feel a bit lost, or maybe you are 29 turning 30 and wondering what you should be doing with your life, or maybe you are in your 40s—like me—and you are thinking, "But I don't have a talent, a *gift*." You are not alone, but we didn't arrive here by mistake. Schools and the world don't tell us that we should listen to our inner self and locate our gift. We are told, "Do well in school, get good grades, do well on "the" test, get into a good college, and get a good job and all will be good." But, if you are feeling like there should be something more, you are probably right. The problem is that few people will respond to this longing and most will settle for "good."

When I was a young boy, I was always finding ways to be creative. I would make costumes from newspaper; take scissors and tape to transform the local paper into a wardrobe for a king or native chief. I would draw pictures on scratch paper for hours and turn cardboard boxes into a home. Like most kids, I enjoyed my gift without needing to be taught what to do—I just created.

When I was 5 years old I received a coloring book and a box of Crayola crayons. I spent hours coloring each page perfectly. Normally, I would be bored with coloring someone else's picture after just a few minutes, because I could create my own from a blank page. But I had an idea to turn that coloring book into something else, just as I had with the newspaper and cardboard boxes. Something told me what I needed to do was share these pictures with the world. So, when I finished coloring each one I cut them out of the book as carefully as a five-year-old can and told my mom that I was going to sell my "paintings". It was the 70s so I embarked on my own going door-to-door selling my art for twenty-five cents—a bargain, I thought. When I knocked on the doors I told people that I was an artist and I was selling my one-of-a-kind "paintings". I knocked on many doors before I found someone home. I was excited when I made my first sale, then my second. I continued door to door until I was nearly sold out. I went to one house with a beautiful garden out front and knocked on the door and a kind lady in a painting smock opened the door with a paintbrush in her hand. I told her the spiel, that I was an artist and selling my paintings. She told me that she was also an artist and she invited me in to see her art. She had the most beautiful oil paintings of the seaside landscape of the cliffs in Santa Cruz where we lived. I was amazed that they appeared to almost leap from the page . . . they were beautiful. She gave me a glass of lemonade and a cookie and asked about my art. I showed her my butterfly "painting", which I was particularly proud of, and she said that she thought I did a nice job of coloring in the lines and choosing the colors, which I noticed too. She chatted for a bit as I finished my lemonade, then I thanked her and walked home. I left a bit sad because I realized that she hadn't offered to buy my butterfly painting. I didn't need the money, I don't even think I knew much about what my twenty-five cents would buy, but I wanted the world to see what I created.

Looking back I realize that what she gave me was far more valuable than all of the others who purchased my art; she shared her gift with me. She invited me into her home, her community—the community of the artist. She valued that we were both creators and she understood the power of a gift; giving something to the world.

"Our gift creates meaning and a meaningful way to connect to the world, to be part of a tribe of givers."

— SETH GODIN, Tribes

You may still be asking, "How do I know what my gift is?" Your gift doesn't equal your talent. Maybe you are a talented painter, but your gift might be to teach or inspire others to paint or to appreciate art or take a chance to create. Your gift can be discovered and cultivated. Everyone has a gift, something to give to the world. Your gift comes from reaching back to your childhood and thinking about the things you did when you were five. Looking at the things that are passions for you, the things that interest you. It is entirely possible that your gift is sitting quietly in your past waiting for you to reignite the passion you once had. If you don't know what your gift is you need to do some self-discovery, try something new, connect to a passion, discover a hobby or interest.

Play has a big role in discovering your gift. Yes, play! Play has no consequences; it's meant to be enjoyable. How you play reflects how you live. If you say, "I don't play anymore," you are losing out on an opportunity to grow and learn about yourself. Plato, the Greek Philosopher said, "You can discover more about a person in an hour of play than in a year of conversation."

"In order to learn about your passions," says Brian at *Roadtrip Nation*, "is to think back to when you were 5 years old. Think about the things you loved to do. Did you love to build things with Legos, or take things apart? Did you love spending time with your mom cooking, or with your dad fixing the car? Did you love to sing and dance. What general things did you enjoy? Write about this time in your life and you will begin to discover your passion." When I was 5, my favorite things were creating things and selling them (an entrepreneur at 5). Now I create ways to help people to discover what they love, what they are meant to do.

ACTION: Take 5 minutes and write down what you spent your young life doing. Maybe it was being outdoors and running and playing with friends or reading books and acting them out.

Remembering your childhood play speaks volumes about who you are and how you play will reveal a glimpse into your gift. It may not be obvious, at first, but don't try to think of your gift; just write down what your five-year-old self liked to do. What are your thoughts about drawing or making colorful images (using crayons or markers) that come to mind when you reflect on the things you did in childhood that brought you joy? Images and colors are often more powerful than black and white words.

Chapter 2

Creativity, Discovery and Passion

"I have no special talents. I am only passionately curious."

—*Albert Einstein*

We as humans are creative beings with an instinctive desire to discover and explore. If you watch young children explore something new such as an unfamiliar space, an empty box or a new toy, they will often approach it with genuine intrigue. There is something built in us that drives us to search, explore, and investigate. We look for new discoveries and ways to do things, sometimes just for fun. When we were young we played and it served as an integral part of our discovery. Kids love to play. For children, play is innate. They invent games that require complex rules and involve their peers. They see it as a good investment of their time and spend hours devoted to carrying out these games, not just merely inventing ways to imitate adult life but attempts

11

to make meaning of their world and the people connected to them.

I remember spending long summer afternoons playing hot lava monster, kick the can, and hide and seek. Somewhere along the way, like most adults, I abandoned play. It might seem easy to say, "Well that's because I grew up." That might be true, but before I grew up, if given the choice, I would have played and discovered all day long. But in contrast, schools forced us to sit still and listen, despite our longing to get outside to play, laugh and explore. Schools, by their nature, constrain and limit play for young children, which is the wrong thing. Schools build compliance, conformity, and status quo. Play, however, is where you discover who you are, your likes and interests. It's even where you first learn to negotiate relationships.

Schools were built to keep kids contained, deliberately away from play and discovery. Have you ever wondered why? Whether teachers and schools know it, there was initially a mission to squash play. There was, and maybe still is unknowingly, a mission to teach conformity and compliance. Play does not fit into that mold. Sure, teachers allow students to play on occasion or have recess, but it's merely to allow for students to let go of energy that makes managing classrooms difficult. It's not because play is recognized as being an important part of learning.

The Industrial model of education was not built to foster creativity. In fact, the industrial model has a mission of compliance. Bells in school establish clear beginnings and endings of a period, similar to a shift in a factory. Even the short break and condensed lunch also mimic the factory model. The industrial model of education doesn't want or need you to be creative or have passion, it needs you to do tasks you were assigned to do over and over. They need you to focus on what they are trying to indoctrinate you with. Be a good student, compliant, so that you can someday be a good, compliant worker. When Henry Ford built his factory and needed to hire more workers than ever to run his industrial machine, he didn't want to slow production, he wanted to make sure the assembly line kept moving, just as students move from class to class, with just minutes between periods. Schools weren't developed to create the best individual, but to provide big business with workers.

Most adults think of creativity as an unnecessary skill that you don't really need, unlike math, reading or writing. I often hear people say, "I am not very creative." What they typically mean is that they forgot how to be creative or don't really see the value in it. By our very nature, humans are creative. It is what enables us to look at something and imagine it to be something that it is not, something new. To see sand and imagine glass, to see a piece of wood and imagine paper, to see a blank piece of paper and imagine a book or a piece of art or plans for a house. All these things were the result of creativity. Imagine a world without the creative spirit. It is this creative spirit that drives us to find our passion.

I was recently talking with my daughter and she was upset because a volleyball camp that she wanted to attend with an Olympic athlete was cancelled. When I explained to her that she shouldn't be so upset, there would be other camps, she said, "Dad, I finally found something that I am passionate about, It's hard to find something I really want to do more than anything. I really want to be a volleyball player. I know that now. It took me a while to discover it but now that I have it I can't stand to see it not happen. I used to think that it was all about academics, because that is what all my friends are focused on, but volleyball drives me."

This struck me because she had to break away from what everyone else was doing and even what she was previously thinking to find her passion. Passion doesn't necessarily follow the rules; it is connected to an emotional part of us that drives us to explore. This year my daughter has played on three different teams, attended two volleyball camps, and has had two personal, one-on-one coaches. These were all her ideas and she pushed me to help her achieve. Even as a fifteen-year-old girl she knows how important passion is. She also knows that discovering this passion wasn't easy. She has played many sports over the years—tennis, swimming, soccer, basketball and track—but none of them fueled her to keep going like volleyball. What if she had given up after playing just one sport? She might have never discovered her passion if she hadn't been persistent to keep trying. What have you given up on or stopped pursuing in your life because you doubted yourself or assumed that you just weren't good enough?

What Will You Discover Next?

Have you ever said, "I am not creative," or "I am not an artist," or "I am not good at math," or "I am not a science person"? Maybe you have always loved to write, like I have, but were told you were no good. Maybe not directly, but perhaps you received a "C" on a story or essay in school and that was enough to persuade you. Our system of education has convinced us that we should be corralled into science, art, math, sports, etc. We have made taking risks and failing at something a negative thing and even punish students for trying. Maybe you have always been drawn to some area but didn't feel like you could accomplish it so you gave up dreaming and trying years ago. You need to silence those limiting beliefs and start to discover and ignite those passions that have perhaps been locked away.

I recently watched a documentary about a young Dutch woman, Laura Dekker, a girl who had a dream to sail around the world, alone. She first sailed alone from Holland to England at thirteen. She made her dreams known to her Dad, who she lived with, and he told her if she wanted to do it she would need to plan it all out on her own. So she studied charts and Google Earth to plan her routes. Carefully studying the waters and safe passages. She wrote to companies and requested sponsorships for equipment. As she was planning her trip the government learned of her plans and threatened to take her away from her father because they viewed sailing unaccompanied as an act of endangerment, totally crazy, and not possible. The court battle ensued but she planned as if she was going anyway. Ten months later, in August 2010, the government agreed to allow her to sail and she began her two-year voyage around the world; not a follow boat, nor a support team accompanied her.

What struck me about Laura Dekker's trip was that she didn't just want the record of being the youngest person to sail around the world; many others had tried, but she wanted to see the world. To see and experience the world was the purpose of her trip, to experience the world up close. In August of 2012, Laura became the youngest person to sail around the world alone, traveling 27,000 nautical miles, spending 519 days at sea. Her dream seemed impossible, even crazy, to everyone else, but Laura and her commitment to those dreams brought her vision to life. Her passion ignited her desire to learn, discover, and do. Discovery is doing— it's an act, not an intellectual pursuit. Being passionate is not merely being interested. You know you are passionate when you get the drive to complete or achieve something regardless of the obstacles. Passion is not just acquiring skills and knowledge about the topic, but doing it, living it. Many people have skills and even immense talent, but just because you have those things doesn't mean you are passionate about it. I know there are tons of people with a lot more knowledge and talent that could write or have written about the same topic as this book you are reading, but I wanted to write it and be successful sharing it with the world, despite all of the barriers that were in my way. Discovery might be doing something new altogether or focusing on the one thing that brings you life and happiness. Chasing your dreams sparks a passion that can ignite an intense life of tremendous fulfillment.

Once you discover what your passion is you can grow and learn. Child-like discovery is fun and exciting, unlike most people's jobs, which are draining, uninteresting and boring. Yes, some of you might be saying that not all work is interesting or exciting, and that life is hard. Well, if you want to live that way that's your choice but I know plenty of people who make a living pursuing their passions. Let those people who don't think it's possible to make a living doing something they love think that, but you don't have to. You can dream and live the life you've always dreamed of having.

Our work life should be just that, life. Our work should place us in such a place of flow that we don't even realize that time passes. It should not seem like work, but pleasure. We should feel connected to the world through our work, giving away our gift because that is what we are called to achieve.

The awesome thing about the connected world we live in, is it is much easier to discover the world than it's ever been. We are a part of the Connection Revolution where we can get online and instantly connect, discover, reach out, and pursue what we love. Online we can discover a tribe of like-minded people, we can seek to create something for an audience, and get immediate feedback. People thousands of miles away are just waiting to connect and hear about what you have to say and share. We have no excuse, we need to just take the first step and declare we are doing something big and then go do it! Do not be afraid to fail. Nothing great started out that way so go ahead and try.

My son has taught me a lot about digital discovery; he loves art and has drawn every opportunity that he gets since he was able to hold a pencil. Unlike his sister, who struggled to identify her passion until recently, he has known all along that he loves to create art. As a young boy he would draw for hours on end. Once he discovered that you could create art with more than a pencil or paints he searched online for more types of art. He has taught himself (with the help of digital master teachers) how to sculpt, paint, draw comics, costume design, create special effects makeup, use Photoshop, learn graphic design, film editing effects and the list goes on. For him, digital apprenticeship works. He finds someone he admires, listens to their tutorials and gives the art a try. He finds the person that's a master practitioner and learns from them, subscribes to their RSS feed (their digital updates), YouTube channels, and watches their tutorials or interviews. If he can find them, he takes an online class. He is passionate about learning, though he dislikes school. I used to tell him to get off the computer and stop surfing the Internet until I realized and saw the profound work that he was producing from watching these tutorials. I was so impressed with his work, that when he says he needs some art supplies we jump in the car and head to the local art store. I don't buy him video games or electronic gadgets, he has to save for those or receive as a gift from family, though he does have some. I won't just give him money to buy "stuff" that he rarely plays with or uses, but the things he needs to fuel his passion I provide in an instant. We need to have the equipment of the profession we are trying to learn about and we need to use it. It shouldn't be in the closet, like my 35 mm camera I was certain was going to be in my hands 24/7 when I got it.

My son is the kind of kid that when he wants to be good at something he won't stop until he learns it, masters it. His passion is now driving his dreams to work in a field that fuels his soul. He is currently working on starting an online apparel company and he's 17 years old. His passion led him to the top leader in the special effects industry that he admires (more about how he did that in future chapters).

What will your passions lead you to do? What is your passion? What if you don't know what your passion is or how to narrow your interest down to things you are passionate about?

That's what the next few chapters are about—finding your passion, separating your passion from your interest. Maybe you are like me and seem to bounce around from idea or interest area and can't seem to focus or get serious about anything or ever complete something you start. Maybe you do complete a few things, but those things seem like such drudgery that even if you started enjoying it, by the time you get near finishing it you hate it. I am convinced you might just be confused or uncertain about your passion. You might be assuming that things you are interested in are your passion, but I am here to tell you they may not be. Passion is something once ignited is hard to contain or stop, you just need to identify it and then ignite it and watch it grow!

Chapter 3

The Art of Failure

"I have not failed. I've just found 10,000 ways that don't work."

— *Thomas A. Edison*

Why do we run from failure? When we attempt something and it doesn't go well we cringe, hoping for something other than failure. We need to view failure differently if we want to succeed in building a life that is built around our passions. We have to believe and accept that we will fail. We should not try to avoid failure, we should just learn to minimize the impact by taking risks that are low level and don't involve losing too much. "Fail soon and often," is a mantra at IDEO, a design firm whose mission is to help companies solve problems. First, let me tell you a bit about why you are conditioned not to know what to do when failure comes knocking at your door.

We are taught in school to not fail, and in fact our entire education system does not promote or encourage failure. Grades are based on showing not that you've learned, but rather that you did not fail. An "A" is supposed to mean mastery in a subject or that you know the expected content, but it doesn't measure learning. You can get an "A" and never learn a thing, maybe you just memorized everything you needed for the test and a week later forgot it all. A good grade is supposed to show that you can perform or demonstrate or deliver the expected outcome, but what it teaches us is that failing is bad, avoid it at all costs. On the contrary, what you need to learn is that failure is GOOD and is not a negative thing, when done at the right time.

The kids that figure out the system of avoiding failure do well in school, but not always as well in life. Students learn quickly that those who do not learn the "game" suffer the wrath of the system—detention, maybe even summer school. All of it equals "FAILURE." This measurement system was designed at the height of the industrial revolution. Creating compliant workers that could perform menial tasks over and over, without question, the exact tasks required. No improvisation, no improvements nor alterations, was the desired outcome. You can't manufacture the same thing over and over again at faster rates if you have someone trying to change things.

I learned this first-hand one summer when I took a job at Plantronics, a technology manufacturing company, when I came home for the summer after my freshman year at college. Our task was to assemble headsets that were used by call centers. Place the cases together, twist the wires, slide them in packages, place the stickers on the keypads, etc. I arrived with the gaggle of workers before the sun rose and left when it was setting. Twelve-hour shifts with breaks and lunches but no windows, no music and no talking. The shift manager would have hourly check-ins to show our productivity. I was often chastised for making the others laugh, which in my mind eased the monotony of the work. Needless to say, I did not last long there. Compliance has never been my strong suit, but I still wasn't prepared to deal with failure the way I needed to be, not from school anyway.

I learned how important failure was when I decided to open a gym in my mid 30s. I thought that buying a franchise was the "safest" route to success and I joined a well-established, successful CEO who had proven success in a different market and who was certain he had the makings of a fitness empire. If we were to join him we could be too.

Boy was I wrong. I didn't see the many warning signs that the CEO was corrupt and not really delivering until it was too late. I should have pulled out of the whole thing, cut my losses and left, but I didn't want to "fail" so I pushed forward. Because I didn't know how to fail, instead of losing $15,000 I ended up losing much more, and eventually had to file for bankruptcy. That was obviously not in my plans at all.

If you are afraid to fail, it's understandable, but you need to begin to let go of a system that has trained you to respond to it, even when you are not in school.

The "schooling for all movement", or common schools, were created because of the need for mass production and compliance. It was no coincidence that this occurred with introduction of the mass production of the Model T and the end of WWI, when what was needed were workers that could do the job they were given. Basic reading and writing and arithmetic, the 3 R's, were all created to ensure workers could meet the minimum requirements.

In 1910, for example, 9% of Americans had a high school diploma. Once the need for a compliant workforce grew, high school diplomas rose. The things that were needed for factories were the things that made up a high school diploma. There was a high value on memorizing, following direction and basic literacy. Risk avoidance and following the status quo and understanding the penalty for failure.

Though we give lip service to the notion of "lifelong learning," we prefer students to do what they are told, not what they think is valuable. Schools created the imminent fear of failure so that no one would break away from the model. The mantra is work hard, be ritually compliant if necessary, get good grades, get into a good college, and get a good job. In the past if you followed this model you would have the American Dream and be "happy." This was true for decades (at least the part about going to college and getting a good job), but unemployment for college graduates has been on the rise since 2007 and in 2013 it was 36.7%.

The future of American job growth will not come from an Industrial Economy. The jobs that disappeared in 2008 when the recession hit, are not going to return now that the economy is on the rise. We are now in the era of the "Connection Revolution" according to Seth Godin and many other pundits. The world needs more people to take risks, pick themselves up, and even fail at times in order to grow new economies. We need a world of creators, not mere consumers.

The 1970s–1990s were labeled the "me" generation—it was all about the individual, how far you could climb the corporate ladder and get ahead, and in fact you were recognized for it. It was all about what grades you got, what school you got into, where you worked. The current generation needs more collaborators, givers, and fewer lone wolves.

Stephen Foster of ThoughtStem, Inc., a company created by 3 PhD students who want to make computer programming the fourth "R" and give access to all, says "that though it might be thought that coding is an individualized activity, tends to be done in pairs or teams in the real world." Stephen says, "coding is rarely done in isolation." His organization aims to teach young coders this from the very first day— it's not all about coding, it's about collaboration. Talented programmers are valued only when they are able to work with others.

Students aren't learning this type of collaboration in school, they are just asked to do what they are told. They are punished when they try to collaborate, or "cheat." Teachers often tell me that when giving students an assignment, the students say, "just tell me what I have to do to get an A." They don't want to learn, they just want to work the system, and it's the system's fault for rewarding this behavior.

Instead of penalizing students for failure, we should show them how to fail—how to learn from it; how to feel; next steps to try again, adjust or just abandon a project that doesn't work. We should be taught how to accept, and even anticipate, failure. In fact, failure is often the only time students learn from their mistakes. It's no wonder that "grit" is a buzzword in education. Teachers aren't typically allowed to think for themselves, choose their curriculum, or even change the scope of what they teach from day to day. What the world needs are creators, inventors, innovators, and students that think for themselves with others to solve problems, or create something that makes the rest of our lives worth living. We need risk-takers, boot-strappers and people who can accept critique (and in fact seek it out). The world needs people with passion to create for the rest of the world, people to find their gift. We need people to embrace the art of failure and try new things, things that they love and care about.

One of my professors in college, Peter Sellars, the world-renowned opera director, said at our graduation commencement at the school of the arts at UCLA that parents are probably wondering, "what will my student do with this creative degree?" There are no jobs for them, no professions. But he reminded the parents that the rest of us work hard our whole lives to appreciate and acquire the things that creative people design, invent, paint, and curate. We buy paintings, go to movies, decorate our homes and buy beautiful cars—all designed by creators. The truth is the rest of society works to celebrate and appreciate the artist—the creators among us.

What is keeping you from doing what you love? From taking a risk and trying something new or reconnecting to a passion from childhood? More than likely it is your fear; fear of failing, fear of not finishing, fear of rejection. Perhaps you fear that things won't turn out they way you planned. Or maybe you have an internal recording inside your head that plays whenever you try to break free. Paulo Coelho, in the book *The Alchemist* wrote, "There is only one thing that makes a dream impossible to achieve: the fear of failure."

The art of failure begins with taking risk, sometimes small at first—learning something new, trying a new food, meeting new people, all help with overcoming fear. I am not saying that every new thing you try will go well, or that you will be an expert at playing guitar in a week, but I bet you could learn at least a song or two. Practicing facing failure is exactly what we all need. What do you have to lose? Now, it's not gambling; don't put everything on the line, such as health, your home, etcetera, but do try. If you wanted to learn piano all your life, what's keeping you from trying? If you have wanted to overcome your fear of public speaking, try joining Toastmasters and grow through your weakness.

Often I thought to myself, *'I should try something new, break away from the status quo, take a risk,'* but I was stuck in the same thinking that I was teaching. I was in education for 20 years, but my generation is plagued with ideas of compliance and fear of stepping out. At first I thought, *'I should go back to school, shift gears, learn something new.'* I soon realized that the skills I needed are not learned on a college campus—they will be taught by the leaders who are making a living doing what they love.

If you are feeling stuck, unable to think what is next in your life, how you will change from the status quo, you are not alone. It's no wonder some of the most successful entrepreneurs didn't complete formal education and ditched the norms. The good news is that it's not too late to learn what the most successful people do to change their mindset and overcome limiting beliefs around change. You can use fear as a motivator to redefine your sense of self-worth. In the next chapter you will learn how the Connection Revolution has made pursuing your passion and dreams easier than ever before in history.

ACTION: Take a risk, try and do something new—sign up for a class, a workshop, or if you are in line at the grocery store and you are uncomfortable, turn to the person behind you and strike up a conversation — the smallest risks sometimes prove to be the biggest first steps to overcoming the fear of failure.

TASK: Ask for a discount at a place that hasn't advertised for a discount. I always say, "Do you have an educator's discount?"

Chapter 4

The Connection Revolution

"Invisible threads are the strongest ties."

—Friedrich Nietzsche

If you went to public school like I did you were showered with the instruction: "Get good grades in school, go to a good college, get a good job." In the current economy jobs are becoming more and more scarce, despite signs of recovery. The bad news is that the coveted jobs that were once here are gone and never returning. However, this is also the good news. Now you may be asking, "How is this good news?" The truth is, who wants a job that puts you in the cubicle with brainless work and an empty promise of a good pension, but in the end lays you off after 20 years of service, too early to retire, and yet no other experience to find a job in a different field?

Maybe you've lost your job and are reading this thinking, "this doesn't sound like good news," but the truth is that it has never been easier to enter into a field that was once hard to enter into. Gatekeepers that once prevented you from getting in the door to a job are now looking for work too. It's time to ditch the career and decide to do what you love doing. The good news is that it's never been easier to pick yourself up and do something that matters. The scarcity of information age is over; the Connection Revolution has arrived.

It has never been easier to get your gift to an audience; you don't need permission to start something or create something for an audience that is waiting for a leader. The Connection Revolution values networking, but not in the same way business once did. People are now connected by more than the country club and golf course. Social media and the Internet have now made it possible to network and give value to people who are thousands of miles away. You can make virtual introductions, share resources, and help people before you ever meet them in public.

Back when I was a kid, there were just three major TV networks that captured America's attention, and only the huge corporations with money could afford to reach this audience and sell something. Today, there are thousands and thousands of ways to find an audience that is waiting to hear from you—YouTube, Netflix, Facebook, Pinterest and future social networks yet to be developed are, and will be, connecting like-minded people together; now everybody has an opportunity to connect with an audience.

If you want to create something, find an audience and say, "Hey I made this, what do you think?" There are dozens of crowd sharing platforms, such as KickStarter and Indiegogo, which have helped people find an audience to launch a business, a product or a film, even before they have all of the money to start the project. You can create an idea and see if there is a market before you spend a dime manufacturing or creating it. You can create a tribe of followers even before you officially launch.

Chris Guillebeau, in his book *The $100 Start Up*, writes that you can't necessarily make a living out of every passion and interest; and perhaps there is some truth to that. Just because you love building with Legos doesn't mean that you can make a living at home in your kitchen building endless creations. But there are people who work at LegoLand in Carlsbad, California that are paid to build with Legos. The question isn't whether you can or can't, it's *how*. It's incredible how passion can fuel a person to create something that was thought by others to be impossible.

Tucker Max, a three time New York Times best selling author, says "Just because you write something doesn't mean you can become a bestseller, you have to have what people want. That's why it's important to find the tribe of people that are looking for what you have to offer.

You Can Make Money Playing Fighting with Sticks?

Every Sunday afternoon, down the street from my house at the park, a large group of men, women and children dress in pseudo armor and hit each other in staged combat scenes that mimic a medieval times dinner and tournament. The activity is called "LARPing" (Live Action Role Play)—think Dungeons and Dragons with real people. They simulate what appears to be scenes from video games. The group was small at first, just a small committed tribe, now there are nearly 60 people and it's growing. I would say that a great gift delivers what the receiver wants and if someone was to create something for this group of loyal followers, they would be ecstatic.

Before iTunes it would have been difficult to get your band in front of an audience, but now, all you need is a simple computer and an Internet connection. With just a few loyal fans you can begin to build something, a tribe. A once hidden group of followers is revealed. All these followers need is a leader, or better yet, a giver—someone willing to put themselves on the line and say, "This is what I have to offer. It's my gift. What do you think?"

The connection revolution has created a shift from mere bystanders glued to network TV willing to be told what to buy, what to wear, and what brand of cereals to eat, into those who demand more. Corporations need thousands, maybe millions, of people to buy their products or watch their shows in order to be profitable, but you and I can be happy with a small, dedicated tribe of followers who want what we have. We don't have huge margins to make up, with large-salaried CEOs with jets and houses in the Hamptons. To create a life that's comfortable and fulfilling, you need to deliver value to those who would listen and they will reward you and sustain your ideal lifestyle because they are connected to you.

If you solve a pain, a problem, or make something easier for your tribe, they will buy, support, or give to your cause. I remember when I was first learning about apps and how they might revolutionize the way that business was done, I heard of a couple that wanted to solve a simple problem. The concept was simple—share your house, a room, or a mattress to provide low cost alternatives to hotels when traveling. Initially people thought that Airbnb was a far-fetched idea. Who would really want to invite strangers into their home and rent a couch? The hotel industry scoffed at the idea and had no concern whatsoever. That is, until Airbnb became a million dollar company and began to eat into the billion dollar hotel industry's pie. Most people would assume that they would fail, but they not only thrived, they are revolutionizing the travel industry and allowing ordinary people to make a living (or at least create income) from sharing their home.

The economy has shifted; just getting a college degree doesn't mean you'll find some great place to work. People should, and will be, asking, "What is your talent, skill or your gift? What is it that you can do, what are you willing give to the world?" In the book *Education of Millionaires: It's Not too Late and It's Not What you Think*, the author says new CEOs are looking for people that can do something to contribute, who can create something, not just those that have knowledge in their head. Each year I was a teacher I would address the parents and have to explain what to expect from my classroom. I would tell them that there is no need to expect their children to memorize the Bill of Rights or the state capitals; they were expected to think about deeper things. Not memorizing history but understanding it for what it is—a series of controversies and interpretations. I wanted my students to think for themselves and think deeply about what they were presented with. Certainly, I wanted the parents to understand that that the skills and thinking of their children required curiosity, questions, collaboration and most importantly, creativity.

What's your excuse for not being a part of the Connected Revolution? What is it that you care about and want to create? If you are still not certain what it is you are passionate about, you need to return to chapter 2 and connect to your interest and find a passion—something that you can commit to learning. Once you find your passion, look for the thought leaders in your area of interest. Connect with them on social media. If they have a podcast, subscribe and listen. If they have a blog, read it and leave value-adding comments. Remember to show up as a giver to the community and the person you are trying to connect with. Think of things that make you unique and find the right way to reach out. Perhaps attend a conference where your leader is speaking and reach out. You can start to use your experience to create a Digital Apprenticeship. Connect with mentors now.

ACTION: Make a list of all of the people with whom you are hoping to make a connection. Then find out all of the ways they are connected online—a blog, a Facebook profile, a podcast, LinkedIn. Be genuine and interact with the community they are connected with. Be responsive—join groups they curate or lead and make contributions to the discussion. If they host an event, attend and make a connection. Do research about your target industry—read blogs, watch YouTube videos, and join in the conversation with notable people in the field or area of which you want to be a part.

Chapter 5

Breaking Away from the Status Quo

"I'm not interested in preserving the status quo; I want to overthrow it."

—*Niccolo Machiavelli*

What is the status quo? The ordinary state of things, not changed or challenged. Most of us are creatures that do not like change; in fact, we fear it. We dislike our job, or situation or cubicle, but we refuse to do anything about it because we say to ourselves, "What if what I try to do ends up worse than things are now?" That's our reason for not challenging the broken system that has educated us, but it shouldn't be what you accept. If you are willing to challenge the status quo, you can change the way you live and fill your life with extraordinary things. If you have purchased this book, my assumption is that you want to figure out how to make a living doing what you love. By the end

41

of this chapter, you will have the strategies, courage, and understanding of how to challenge the areas of your life where you have accepted the status quo.

My daughter Skylar decided at the end of her sophomore year that she had learned as much as she could from the high school she was attending. Though it's one of the most sought after charter schools in the country, she wanted more. She realized that she was loving volleyball more than her other friends and teammates. Unlike her peers, she decided she was driven to focus on her passion in volleyball instead of academics.

She wasn't the best player on the team, nor the tallest, but she was the hardest worker. Her passion for the sport inspires me. In fact, last year she played on three separate volleyball teams and craved even more. This past summer, in her pursuit to grow and learn more about the sport, she researched and secured a private coach all on her own. She interviewed him and began private coaching, at a rate she negotiated, that cost less than a movie and popcorn. Still, she craved more learning and discovered that the local community college was offering a volleyball camp for girls, working with college level players and coaches. She signed up and asked the coach for a discount if she signed up to do both sessions, which they agreed to. While at the camp she met the head coach for the men's team of the junior college. When the coach offered the girls an opportunity to receive more coaching, she was the only one to raise her hand and take him up on it. Again, she confirmed a series of one-on-one coaching sessions for herself and negotiated a rate of $20 an hour with the coach that happens to do all of the college recruiting for the team. Her intention was to learn what coaches look for when they recruit players. Her vigilance to learn and discover immediately began to payoff—just prior to the start of her junior year of high school she entered the varsity team tryouts with newfound confidence and skills, crushed it, and made the team!

She also has a plan to leave high school after her second semester and attend an online school so she can begin traveling and training with the college team as an intern—another opportunity she created. I asked her what her goal ultimately was and she said it's to play volleyball. She wants to play on a college team more than anything else. So much so that she wants to practice with the team whether she gets to play on the court or not. Finishing high school early and trying to make the team has become her short-term goal. Her long-term goal is to play volleyball in college and find a college that will lead her to her passion to study the sciences. Her friends think that missing her senior year of high school seems like a crazy notion. In contrast, she sees it as an opportunity. She has already arranged to workout with the college team at 5:45 AM before school just so she can be included. Half the time she helps keep records and stats for the men's team and the rest of the morning is private coaching. I never told her to do this; she just has passion. Pursuing passion gives us a break away from the status quo and it doesn't require you to have all of the answers. Each opportunity led to another for Skylar; while all of her friends will be playing volleyball in high school as seniors, she figured out a way to be a player of the college team at 16 years old.

Colin Wright was a successful designer, artist, and owner of a graphic design firm in LA right out of college in his early 20s but decided to give it all up to travel the world and live his life the way he determined. According to his book, *My Exile Lifestyle*, he found himself unfulfilled by the status quo so he told his family and friends he was leaving it all behind. Rather than work for clients that demand his work to meet their needs, he designs apparel, writes books, writes a blog and lives a minimalist lifestyle. He publishes the blog www.exilelifestyle.com and his followers vote on the country that he will move to and live in for many months at a time. Colin realized that his future was not what he wanted so he broke the mold and set out on his own journey. Blake Boles, a leader in the "Unschooling" movement, said, "We don't live our lives for school, we live our lives for adventure."

Maybe you have a great job, one that you are good at, one that you are excelling in, a job in which you are climbing up the corporate ladder, receiving praises for your accomplishments, but on the inside you feel empty. You feel empty, perhaps, because your gift is hidden, unshared with the world; maybe it has even been forgotten by you. Have you forgotten what you loved to do when you were five years old? Maybe you've even contemplated changing careers, or thought about going back to school to try something new. Maybe you're asking, "Should I be doing something else?" Maybe you're confused because you don't hate your job, but you still feel like you are stagnant, like still water—not moving, not flowing . . . stuck.

Wanda Sykes, a famous comedian and actress, once said in an interview that her transition from working for the NSA to doing standup comedy was difficult for her parents to accept because she had gone to college. She landed the job at the NSA, but she soon realized that she didn't belong there.

Wanda's gift was making people laugh. It's what she wanted to give to the world. In the beginning it was a struggle. She did comedy part-time, taking the train to New York on the weekends and at night after work to perform at the biggest comedy clubs. One of her most important feats was finding great mentors. Even though everyone else thought she was crazy her mentors cheered her on. When others thought she was taking too big of a risk to give up her job and the security of her cubicle, she followed her passion instead.

Breaking away from the status quo requires you to go against what people think you should do. As the saying goes, "misery loves company", and so do people following the status quo—they don't want others to escape if they have to suffer. Often times even people who mean well will try to steer you away from a dream. The vampires and zombies live in the status quo and want everyone else to be like them—dead and barely living. Avoid the status quo if you want to have a passionate life. Surround yourself with passionate people who encourage you, are living the life you want to live, and can help you get to where you want to be. Remember the adage that you are the average of the five people you associate with the most. Sometimes you have to break away from those who hold you down.

Breaking away from the status quo often means being different and people will tell you that you can't make a living doing what you love. They might say, "Hey, I love eating pizza, but no one is going to give me money to do that, be realistic," which I agree with in part. But you loving pizza is not your gift to the world, it's a pleasure or an interest, but not what you are meant to do. Who knows what your gift might be or how your passions and interests can become something that the world needs. One thing's for sure, you'll never know if you don't try to find it. We must visualize what the perfect day looks like, how it feels, and then pursue it because our desires need our attention.

Malcolm Gladwell wrote in the book *Outliers* that it takes 10,000 hours of practice in order to achieve mastery in a particular field, to become an expert, but I don't know that it is totally true. I think skills and abilities in one area will carryover and apply to another. Tim Ferriss recently said in his podcast *The Tim Ferriss Show* that he disagrees with Gladwell as well. He applied the 80/20 rule, saying that 20% of your effort gives you 80% of the output. He gives the example of acquiring a new language and if you knew 20% of the most important vocabulary for that language it would give you 80% of the ability to speak the language. If you focus on the word "mastery" you tend to shut down and then not move forward. Mastery is a word that doesn't reflect the majority of people who are successful in a particular field, but the elite few. You don't need to be perfect to make a living doing what you love—you need action.

You can hack your way to mastery if you consider that the time spent growing and struggling represents a large number of the hours. A significant amount of time has been wasted by individuals by discovering shortcomings and failures when acquiring a new skill. If you sit at the foot of a master practitioner they can help you accelerate your learning to gain confidence and collective wisdom that these master practitioners share. It's like borrowing their 10,000 hours. Instead of failing on a simple thing for ten hours, get help from a master and move on in ten minutes. The solution is getting connected with a master practitioner.

Many of us believe that it takes a long time to acquire learning because traditional school systems drag things out for longer than they need to be; it's a one size fits all approach. Even if you are ready to move on, you can't leave high school until you're 18 and done serving the twelve-year sentence of school. The truth is that you can exceed and grow much more quickly by learning from a master.

Collaboration vs. The Individual

In school they said no peeking, no cheating, no sharing, no doing each other's work, no collaborating—but that's the exact opposite of how to hack your way to mastery. What if there was another student in the class who mastered the content and was able to demonstrate their mastery by teaching somebody else instead of having to take a test? This would create more mini-instructors and eliminate the wasteful use of testing to manage behavior. In the martial art Judo, practitioners advance when they are ready to take the belt exam to demonstrate their mastery. Not everyone earns their black belt at the same time or in the same way.

Dan Thoene, an Emmy Award winning sportscaster turn teacher, decided to use the principles of Judo to change the way he teaches math. He studied how Singapore (the country who was once almost dead last for mathematics in the world) has risen to the top 10 recently by limiting the number of concepts taught in math from over 180 to focusing only on 12 major disciplines. He focuses on the 20% of the material that gives 80% of the success in math. The entire principle of learning math was shifted from individual to the community–Dan created Judo Math, a better way to teach math, a teaching and learning system that thrives with collaboration and discourages the solo learner. He creates what he calls the "dojo" environment in his classroom, where he uses relationship based learning to develop a community of learners. Dan's gift is helping kids love math and teaching teachers how to get them to love it. His passion for teaching math is now a business that thrives, and he not only inspires students, but teachers around the globe. Check it out at www.judomath.com.

Digital Land Grants

It's never been easier to find a place to share your gift. I have always admired street performers because they put themselves out there. They say, "Here I am, this what I have to offer, take it or leave it." They either get rewarded or they don't but they make their passion and gift public . . . they act with such courage, what about you?

We are living in an era where you can stake a claim in the digital world; set up a place for your gift to live. You can have a digital land grant—domain names for websites are cheap and anyone can have one, but so few are willing to choose themselves and say, like street performers, "Hey World, here I am." Those that invest in putting themselves out there for the world to see will have a future that will return many times over.

What fuels you ... what drives you? Maybe your friend just asked the question: What will happen if you fail? That's a great question, and the truth is that more than likely, it's not life or death. If you fail, it will be time to get up and try again or move on. The world needs you to share your gift. But more importantly you need to share your gift. No one on their deathbed ever said, "I wish I moved up the corporate ladder higher or stayed at the office longer or spent more time in front of TV." Rather, they say, "I wish I would've loved more, had more adventures, or took more risks."

Breaking away from the status quo might mean standing out in the crowd. It might mean that some people think you are crazy, and that's why you need to find a group of people and a mentor that can relate to you in order to help you navigate the challenging waters of doubt.

What is holding you back from stepping out? Make a decision to do something to take a step in the direction of your dreams.

In the remaining chapters you will learn how you can hack your way into any industry even if you don't have any contacts or experience in that field. You will discover how you can find a kick-ass mentor and really start accelerating your learning.

ACTION: Make a list of all of the organizations, meet-ups, groups, classes, and mentors that might be in your area. Join a group and attend a meeting. Don't let the status quo rule you. You have wanted to do something so what's keeping you from acting now?

Make a list of the things that you are passionate about but have been ignoring or just plain forgot about. Next choose the top three that you want to act on. Perhaps you have wanted to audition for a play. Find a local theater troupe or comedy class and sign up. If you love languages and travel, find a group that meets regularly and speaks a language that you want to learn, or brush up on it and plan a trip to that country.

This isn't meant to be a bucket-list with items like "visit Machu Picchu," or "go to the Galapagos Islands," or "sky-dive". This should be a list of things that matter to you. These are things you are passionate about. Things that make you feel alive. Spend five minutes right now; don't think, just write about the things you used to love and want to reconnect with. Ready, set, go!

Chapter 6

Hack Your Learning

"Have no fear of perfection - you'll never reach it."

—Salvador Dali

Do you want to know how to hack your way into any industry? You need the skills discussed in this chapter. Anyone can do it, even if you don't know anyone in that industry and don't have a degree in that field. This chapter isn't for those of you who want to be a doctor or lawyer or any other career that requires a certificate, but you can hack into almost any field if you follow the steps laid out in this chapter.

Learning Snapshot

How does learning happen, anyway? Learning isn't something that can be done *to* us. We only learn when we *choose* to learn. All of us start out as young people with a deep desire to discover, question and learn. We need to return to that

55

state if we want to hack our learning. I want you to think of a moment when you learned something new. Who was there? What were they doing? What were you doing? How did you feel about what you were learning? This significant learning snapshot is important because this is the environment where learning really happens. We are not all the same, but I bet our learning snapshots have many similarities. I would guess that there was an element of excitement, dialogue between the learner and the mentor. There probably was an opportunity to ask questions and a time for imitation and practice. I would imagine that you had some excitement and enjoyment from experiencing an activity you were successful with some coaching from your mentor or peers. I am guessing the experience was one on one, or in a small group. All of these experiences are the foundation of the apprenticeship model and will need to be replicated if you are going to hack your way into a new industry.

By now you should have identified your area of passion that you want to focus on. Now it's time to put your *Art of Apprenticeship* hacking skills into practice. Remember, in the last chapter we talked about how to hack your learning by getting connected to a master practitioner. Now we are going to talk about how you can acquire this learning once you find a guru who is willing to guide you. You don't need someone to officially say, "Yes, I agree to be your mentor," but learning from a master practitioner is the key to hacking your way into a field that is new to you. You do not have to follow these in order, but they are vital to making significant progress quickly.

Step 1: Connect With Like-Minded People

One of the biggest steps to take when trying to hack your way into a new industry or area is to find a tribe of people that get you, have been there, or are also trying to make their way into something new. Learn as much as you can about your passion topic and connect with those doing the same thing. It might seem intimidating at first but you need to engage and start participating and giving value. Sometimes giving value is just being a part of something; it's okay not to know what you are doing, in fact, being naive can sometimes work to your advantage. A good tribe of people is happy to help someone who is showing initiative and learning from the group. Now, you should also do some homework and know what the group is all about, whether it is an online community or an in-person event; don't show up unprepared. Know as much as you can and then be a willing and humble sponge. Additionally, if you can help others by giving value, that's a plus.

Step 2: Be a Grateful Giver

When you first connect with a group, find ways to give and add value to the community and its leaders before you take from them. If you sign up for a conference or training and you are new to the topic of the conference, find a way to be the one that helps connect people or deliver value. For example, I wanted to make a transition to the online world, something I knew nothing about, so I joined Pat Flyyn and Chris Ducker's group *1 Day Business Breakthrough* mastermind group. I had no established business, or even a good idea, and wanted to give to this great group of entrepreneurs. With the aim of adding value, I connected with everyone and orchestrated a pre-conference happy hour the day before the mastermind event. My goal was to help those who could make it have the opportunity to become introduced and make meaningful connections before the actual event. I arranged the time, the location, and sent invitations to facilitate and encourage the gathering. As a result, I became viewed as a connector and a person that was a giver to the community.

Step 3: Hold Yourself Accountable

Find a buddy to help you stay on track with outcomes. Set up a regular time to meet, either in person or online, and don't make excuses for not meeting if you haven't done anything. The pressure of accountability is the reason you are having the meeting. Set clear goals for the next meeting and check in via email or by phone. Be sure to pick someone that is going to ask you questions that drive you towards your goal.

Step 4: One Passion at a Time

Only study what you are truly passionate about. Don't chase money. If you are really going to learn something from someone you need to have genuine interest. People can sniff out a con pretty easily. If you don't care enough about the topic, return to your passion list and figure out what really makes you excited.

Step 5: Choose Clear Outcomes

If you are like many entrepreneurs, you have a hard time focusing on one thing; you have so many ideas that you can't execute them fast enough. Narrowing your choice to one outcome may be difficult because you fear the one you pick might be the wrong one. The challenge for you will be to stay focused on just one until you finish it. Don't get paralyzed thinking too much. Just make a simple plan and act on it.

Step 6: Connect with Top Leaders

Connect with those in your area of interest by reading their blogs or forums and attend conferences that they attend. Don't just look for famous people, look for doers—those living passionately the way you want to live. Just because they are a leader at the top of their field doesn't mean they are living with the most passion. Be wary of chasing people based on some ranking alone.

Step 7: Plan a Public Display of Learning

Make it known that you are learning something new and share that with the world. Making a commitment to your development and learning requires humility, so choose to be vulnerable and tell people that you are learning piano and then decide to have a public recital or agree to play at a party. Make it real so that there are meaningful reasons to learn. Learning for learning's sake won't serve you, if you choose not to share it with the world. Don't fool yourself into thinking, "Well, I can keep practicing." The reason you are practicing a new skill is so that you can hack your way into a new industry. If you want to work as a wedding or event planner, volunteer your skills at a wedding for a friend or post it on Craigslist. If you are interested in working in film, look for gigs online and be a member of a student film crew. If you merely learn without public practice, then learning has no practical meaning.

Do Not Be a Lifelong Learner

You need to think of learning as a quick path to living the life you desire. Learning in school usually had no real world application—you studied for a test and then promptly forgot the material. But, if you want to hack your way into any industry, you need to apply your learning quickly. The only way to measure if you've succeeded at being a lifelong learner is to wait until you die. The truth is, schools were created to serve the needs of businesses not the individual. They were created to serve the industrial machine. Thomas Jefferson said that the purpose of education is not to serve the public but to create one, so you taking control of your learning is a great act of democracy.

Why Schools Didn't Teach You to Learn

What's wrong with schools? It's the place that students are placed against their will and forced to "learn" something that may not seem valuable or may never serve them. For me, school was that place where it was okay for adults to say, "this isn't useful now but trust me, it will be someday." Elementary school was supposed to prepare us for middle school, middle school for high school, and high school for college. It's not until you get into a good college that you realize you didn't really need most of what they told you was important.

One of the ways you can regain your learning is to begin to think about your passions and interests. When you connect to the one thing that you are passionate about, you can't help but chase it down until you are living the life that you love. The funny thing is that when you were in kindergarten, you started with this deep desire to play, discover, question, and genuinely share with the world what you made. You need this simple but important quality if you are going to hack your way into a new industry.

Be Like a Kindergartener

We need to return to the curious state we were in when we were five years old. We did what made us happy; we played, we danced, we explored. I want you to think of a significant moment when you were five years old. Think of something you learned or loved doing. Think of when you really learned something—not just facts, but something that really sticks with you now. What were you doing, who was there, what did you do? I want you to think of all the things that were around you. How did you feel when you learned what you did? This significant moment is important because the environment where learning really happens for you can be identified in that activity. Did you learn most one-on-one or in a group? Was somebody teaching you a new skill? Who was the most important person during the learning moment? Was there a test or practice involved?

I bet some of your significant learning moments have some similarities to mine. I bet there was dialogue, the ability to ask questions and opportunity for trial and error. There was probably time for practice and then time to get some coaching or mentoring and a chance to try it again. It was learning by doing it for pleasure and enjoyment while you experienced it. It was probably a small-group, not many people involved. These are the qualities that are important to all of us when we learn something great.

Anti-School is Pro-learning

Maybe you have been thinking that you should go back to

school lately because your job is sucking the life out of you, but instead I want you to think about hacking your education. I know that it may seem like I'm anti-learning but I am not. I am against wasting valuable time in most schools, which are a part of a broken and antiquated system. The idea of creating your own learning is what's most important. The most significant learning you ever do is the learning you decided for yourself. There is a reason that so many students are in school but really do not love learning. I support the whole "uncollege" movement—the tribe of people who are saying, "we want more from our education . . . we want more from high school, from college."

Dale Stephens, a Thiel Foundation Fellow founded an entire movement whose mission is to help young people create their own destiny through their own self-directed learning. Stephens founded the website http://Uncollege.com which provides support to people who are thinking they would like to take a gap year and define their success by starting something, rather than going to college. Dale's participation as a Thiel Fellow allowed him to work alongside some of the world's most creative and motivated young people; a Thiel Fellowship helps them bring their most ambitious projects to life. Thiel Fellows are given a grant of $100,000 to focus on their work, their research and their self-education while outside of university.

Peter Thiel, a venture capitalist, entrepreneur, and co-founder of PayPal, each year has given 20 people under 20 years old $100,000 to take a year off school and start something big. He provides these young fellows with a community of visionary thinkers, inventors, scientists and entrepreneurs who provide guidance and business connections that can't be replicated in any classroom.

Learn more about this at http://www.thielfellowship.org. If these twenty-somethings can make plans to change the world, so can you.

Chapter 7

Pick Yourself

"Try not to become a man of success. Rather become a man of value."

—*Albert Einstein*

The best part of college for me was getting my first internship. I remember I had just moved to Los Angeles and dreamed of working in the film industry. I had virtually zero experience in film, but I knew how to use a program called WordStar. In the days before Windows, this DOS-based word processing system required users to practically memorize every function with keystrokes in order to perform basic operations like centering a text or bolding a word. I was able to score an internship at a production company working directly with the executive producer because I knew how to do a mail merge on WordStar. It was pretty special because the intern before me was David Koepp, the screenwriter of Jurassic Park. This was my break. I learned so much in such a short period of time, mainly how to navigate the Hollywood system and how everything works, at ten times the pace of my peers in film school who were busy studying the film industry in books.

No one told me to go look for an internship, I just decided that it was what I needed if I was going to learn about how production companies work. I was not a film major but I knew that I should use my talents to try and make my way in and it worked for me. It can work for you too. You need to stop waiting for permission and pick yourself; don't expect there to be a big announcement stating "It's your turn!"

Learn as much as you can about your passion and connect with those doing the same thing. I worked so hard to get into a good school and when I arrived I was disappointed that it was all lecture and memorization. Internships allow for so much learning and so much opportunity to fail and grow; it was the best thing for me, I grew up in my internship. School seemed so much like a waste of time and by my second quarter I was totally bored. It wasn't because I wasn't smart, or the fact I'm dyslexic and school has always been a struggle for me, but it was more because no real learning happened in my general education classes.

My freshman year I convinced the chair of the Spanish and Portuguese department that I might declare those as my major just so I can live abroad and attend the university in Guadalajara while still receiving credit at UCLA. By the end of my sophomore year I received a letter from the school stating that since I was starting my junior year I needed to declare my major. So I looked at every program and searched for the major that could fit all my courses and give me credit and I finally found one—a small program with 20 people called "World Arts and Culture." It was perfect. Every single class fit exactly into the ideology of a broad generalization for schooling. I was still on track to graduate in four years even though I had taken time off on several occasions.

My previous internships led to many other non-paid positions that gave me far more experience and opportunity than my peers who chose to get their learning from classroom lectures and notes alone.

An important lesson I learned was that there was no one waiting to choose me. If I were to succeed, I needed to do something; I needed to take a step and pick for myself. I was really shy and not the strongest academically, but I worked extremely hard and always found a way into a new position. The film industry didn't care where you went to film school;

they just wanted to know that you had skills that added value. I needed to be like that little boy again who was going door-to-door telling people: "Here I am. I'm an artist. Buy my paintings. Pick me." If I can do it, so can you.

A Lesson in Magic

My partner and I were walking home from watching a World Cup match in our neighborhood. As we rounded a corner near home, we saw a little boy with a sign made of cardboard that read "Magic trick one dollar." His head low, his chin to his chest, I don't even think he noticed us at first standing in front of him. I couldn't help but notice that he was about the same age that I was when I was peddling my paintings door-to-door. "I want to see your magic trick," I said. His head rose and his blue eyes beamed.

He quickly dropped the sign, picked up his magic wand, which was sitting at his feet, and he opened a box to reveal a quarter. He said, "I'll make this quarter disappear!" Quickly, he closed the box and said "Abracadabra!" I was glad to hear that the same magic words from my youth still worked. He waved the wand over the box and then opened it. To his dismay, the quarter was still there. He sighed, looked up at us and declared that it doesn't always work the first time and he tried again. The young boy closed the lid, waved his magic wand again and this time it worked—the quarter had vanished. I think he was just as amazed as we were. "Wow," I said, "that's a great trick." My partner and I each gave him a dollar. The boy was so excited he put the wand and the box down on the sidewalk and picked up the sign with a renewed sense of determination. We went on our way and he stood there waving his sign. His smile filled the street.

That boy didn't do what every other kid was doing, setting up a lemonade stand like the thousands of other kids before him; he decided he wanted to use his gift, to do his own thing, to share with the world his talent. His message was loud and clear: pick yourself.

It would have been more logical to go with what works: make a lemonade stand. It would have been easy to make the assumption that no one would give him money for a magic trick, but he decided to delight the world with his gift.

Silence the Committee

If you are like me, you struggle with self-sabotaging thinking on a regular basis. I have voices in my head that tell me that there's no way that this will work, no matter what I do. The voices I hear say I am not good enough or nobody will care or listen if I put myself out there. Maybe you're not like that, but perhaps you can relate to what I'm talking about. I call the logical, but non-helpful group of people in my head, "The Committee." The Committee often gets together and has a conversation in my head. One Committee member will say "I have a good idea listen to this," and then another Committee member will say "Are you crazy, he tried that last time and it didn't work!" The loud committee member chimes in, "Remember when he tried to start the gym but it ended up in bankruptcy?" Or still another, "Remember all those times he started businesses and he never got any-where? Do you really think this will be any different?"

This banter continues inside of my head until I am para-lyzed and do nothing as a result. Those negative voices that form The Committee are the ones I have to silence if I want to be successful because they are the voices of doubt. If you have ever had The Committee in your head you must tell them, "Shut up! It's my life and I will succeed!"

Learn to be Immune to Rejection

I've learned more from my failures than I have from my successes but rejection feels so much harder than success. Sometimes we don't pick ourselves because we are afraid of being rejected. I've learned that rejection is not about me. Rejection is just one more chance to find the right person for your gift. If you want to succeed you need to realize rejection is just a way of selecting the right audience. If someone doesn't think your idea is good, that's fine; it's not for them. Your gift is good for the right person.

Schools don't prepare you for rejection, they teach you how to avoid it. The very system that is supposed to educate you and make you aspire to be a lifelong learner actually penalizes you for failing and trying something new.

Don't Wait for an Invitation, Start Now!

Find your gift. Rediscover it if you've lost it and do something to cultivate it. Use your gifts to change the world. If you're happy with your job and you love it, that's great, then press on, perhaps this book is not for you. But if you want to start something new, something that ignites your passion and you have yet to acquire the job you desire, you will need the help of a master practitioner. The next several chapters will help you prepare, teach you how to set up your own apprenticeship, select a leader to learn from and start doing what you love. One thing I know for sure is that you can create a life that's filled with passion and you can make a living doing something you love. I have and it started with taking the first step to write this book. Just because you're good at something or good at your job doesn't mean you should keep doing it unless you're happy doing it. Let your passion fuel you. If you don't love what you do, or if you feel like you should be doing more than just working, or you are just waiting for the weekends to come, or that once a year vacation—you need to pick yourself now, silence The Committee, and discover the gift you know you want to share with the world.

Pick yourself because you no longer have to wait to be chosen. There was a time when the world would only get to know you when the "Powers That Be" called your name. If you were lucky enough to be on a show like Johnny Carson or Star Search, perhaps you could get discovered, but today, getting seen or heard doesn't require a panel of TV judges or a gong. If you are waiting for the right time, it is now. Start something—you don't need permission.

Chapter 8

Finding Your Kick-Ass Mentor

"Don't let what you cannot do interfere with what you can do. "

—*John Wooden*

Finding a mentor is more about building a reciprocal relationship than it is about building some formal arrangement for learning. Since the nature of apprenticeship is a tacit relationship, you might be surprised by how accessible people are when you are able to connect and add value.

Finding leaders to learn from is one of the most important steps to achieving your dreams. Some things you will learn on your own, from your own mistakes, and some things you should learn from the mistakes of others. Allow leaders to see the real you so they can relate to you. Most people are afraid to pursue their dreams for three reasons: (1) they are afraid that they will not achieve what they set out to do, (2) they feel that they don't deserve to have success, or (3) they feel that they will be judged by those around them for trying and failing or succeeding.

We look up to Olympic athletes because we admire their skill, passion, and commitment to training. We watch as the coaches inspire them or push them to new heights. I used to just envy great athletes and thought, "If I had a person in my life like that, I'd really be awesome too." It is true and you can have an awesome coach and master teach you. With the Internet and the Connection Revolution, it's easier than ever to connect to those who are doing what you'd like to be doing. Maybe you follow them online or read their blog. Maybe you read about their work or consume their books or you live where they train or do work. A simple email, tweet, or friend request on Facebook might be all you need to start building a relationship with that person. Better yet, find that person's address and do it the old-fashioned way—send a letter to express your interest in their field. Find out about a conference where they are speaking and volunteer to help the organizers. Find ways to connect and stand out.

7 Steps to Find a Kick-Ass Mentor

1. Be a Giver and Not a Taker. Realize that a master in any given field is a busy person. They would love to just stop and help everyone, but the truth is they can't do it. They just don't have the time to give. Find ways to add value to your leader so that when you get an opportunity to connect, you will have already been connected in six degrees of separation. Be influential, contribute and know what your leader or community values. Maybe you connect with somebody that works closely with them and help them in some way; you may find your way to their inner circle through a friend. You would be surprised how small the world really is, especially online.

Ways to Add Value:

- Contribute to their tribe

- Attend conferences they sponsor or attend

- Read their books

- Listen to their podcast

- Respond to comments on social media (Twitter, Facebook, Linked In)

- Participate in their charity of choice

- Know about their history and values

- Help the community that surrounds them either virtually or in person

- Make something worth sharing

2. Create Your Own Digital Apprenticeship. Share with your leader what you are doing. Showing initiative and promise demonstrates how much you care and are dedicated to the area that you are learning. Show up having done some self-development. Don't expect they will be impressed with your passion alone and will just drop everything to help you. Have a learner's attitude. Take a short course in Udemy, Skillshare, Creative Live, Udacity, Khan Academy or any number of free online programs or college courses to help grow in your understanding of a topic. If you don't show interest in your learning, neither will your leader.

3. Imitate Greatness. Study the habits of great leaders and do what they do. Imitation is one of the first steps to growing as learner. If you are not willing to step into their way of thinking it will be difficult to relate. Successful people imitate other successful people.

Apprenticeship is about learning from the small informal things that people do; not the hard skills, but the quieter, soft-skills that often go unnoticed by others. If you read that your leader rises early to work or writes each day before sunrise, give it a try. If they listen to a certain podcast or recommend a book, listen to it or read it, even if it isn't something you would normally choose. One time I read that my leader took cold showers to stimulate their thinking and to get used to feeling uncomfortable first thing in the morning. I thought, "Wow, that's challenging." So, for 30 days I did it too. At first, it seemed impossible, but then each day it got easier and easier. I found that I often avoid being uncomfortable and this exercise helped me to address it everyday. Find something to imitate from your leader so you can stand on similar ground and understand their perspective.

4. Be Humble, Be a Beginner. Colin Wright of exilelifestyle.com says, "Be humble, allow yourself to look ignorant and ask dumb questions." Don't be the guy who always knows the answers or pretends that he does. Experts don't view this as a sign of strength, but rather a sign of arrogance and selfishness. An apprentice relationship is one where the master gives far more than he receives, but it's the time and small added value the apprentice gains from watching and listening to the master that makes the learning curve so dramatic. Some people are at the top of their field, while others remain average, not because they don't possess the same basic skills to do the work of a master, but because they excel in the smallest of improvements overlooked by others. The great practitioners share and give away these subtle things in the informal setting of apprenticeship. Humble people ask questions. If you are changing careers and embarking on a new journey, become a student, be humble. Don't pretend to know it all and put-off the person or group of people who you are trying to connect with.

5. Connect with the 2nd in Command. If you connect with someone that's not the top dog, but is excellent, you will soon have access to the top. Sometimes people feel that they must learn from the top dog or it's not worth their time, but in reality those who are able to influence the leader might be more important than the top person in the field because they know all of the same people but are lesser known, more available, and more accessible. Let's say you want to learn from the top wake boarder in the country. Just sending her an email to say, "Hey, I want to be your apprentice," might not be the best strategy. Instead, maybe find out who her boat driver is, or her protégé, and reach out to them. You might find they are willing and excited to be reached out to and offer to help.

6. Don't Say, "Will You Be My Mentor?" People are generous but they are leery of a commitment that seems to be forever. Rather, ask for some help with a specific question or seek advice in some way from the members of the community that the leader supports. Leaders watch the followers of their tribe closely and they can see if you are a part of the group just to take or if you are there to give and learn. If you get the chance to learn from a master, make it clear, and have a measurable outcome from the request.

Be knowledgeable about the person and their area of interests or expertise.

Learn everything you can about them before you reach out to the person; be savvy. Connect with the person or tribe they are involved in. Learn how they think, what they care about, what they're passionate about, and what causes they endorse. Help those in the community they are a part of, make sure you are active in their blog posts, comments, competitions, etcetera. You have so much to offer even if you know little about the area you want to enter. You are uniquely you. Interact and be a giver.

7. Conquor Your Doubts, Objections and Fears—"Avoid the Zombies and Vampires." Having fears is the sign that you might be on the right path of following your dreams and finding your gift. Finding your Yoda is easier than you think. When you tell people of your plans to do something great or find a great master practitioner and become their protégé they may think you are crazy, strange, or impractical, especially if you are someone who seems to have everything already—the house in the suburbs, two kids, the nice car, the high paying position. They may think you are nuts to leave all this to pursue something else. If people think you have everything that a man or woman could want, or that you are already living the dream, they may try to dissuade you from trying something new or different. You need to avoid these people I call Zombies and Vampires. Zombies are the living dead—they're unhappy with their life and want others to be just as "dead," or not living, as they feel. They move towards you with every reason that you are wrong, they just seem to be after you. There is no rationalizing with them or convincing them you are right. They can't be changed back. Don't try, even if at one time they were just as ambitious as you are now. When people become zombies, it's time to leave them behind. They may have good intentions but they are after your dreams; they will just get in your way.

Vampires, on the other hand, are out for blood. They intentionally try to attack you, drink your blood, and make you—like them—poisoned. They aren't aimless; they are precise and calculated. They will often tell other people to help them to convince you that you are on the wrong path. Vampires are people who have negative things to say about everything you've already tried to do in the past and things related to the future, things you are dreaming of doing. They think everything you do is wrong. Their criticisms are like bites. They see everything you can't do. They will find a way to put you down and tell you that you are on the wrong path. They will never help you to get to where you want to be. They are only happy if you are miserable like they are. They can't be reformed so just run away now. Don't get me wrong, I love my family and friends, but sometimes they are the zombies and vampires to your dreams. Just walk away. Avoid both of these bloodthirsty creatures, especially the vampires. They will crush your dreams before you even get a chance to get underway.

ACTION: Try joining a meet-up group in your area, join a mastermind, attend a conference, connect on Facebook with the online community, and find groups that are like you, who have dreams and want to succeed.

It's never been easier to connect to like-minded people online. "Digital Apprenticeship" is what I call it when you get the opportunity to connect with someone online and learn valuable information, discover new passions, and learn a new skill. My son learned how to sculpt, do creature make-up, special effects editing for video, and tons of other stuff, all from online tutorials and master practitioners he admires.

He appreciates the ability to practice and rewatch all of these techniques over and over before committing to putting his work into the world. This digital apprenticeship is where he watches the subtle things that make the master great.

Mentors can be found in a variety of people and situations; mentors and leaders can be those who are just a few steps ahead of you but are living the dream you seek to have. They have figured out what you are trying to achieve. Remember the steps above and make a decision to find the person(s) with whom you want to connect.

Chapter 9

Why an Apprenticeship?

"Tell me and I forget, teach me and I may remember, involve me and I learn."

—Benjamin Franklin

During the Renaissance, twelve-year-old boys were sent to study under the tutelage of a master artisan. These artists were skilled in painting, woodworking, sculpting, ironworks, engineering, etc. The young apprentice would study the craft by first doing menial jobs to keep the shop clean, such as sweeping or cleaning up the supplies or running errands. Slowly, the apprentice was allowed to help the master with various pieces of the work. In their own time the apprentice would practice the fundamentals, such as sketching samples or building with scraps. As the apprentices grew and demonstrated their ability, they might be asked to take on a small project and the master would critique their work. The subtle changes are what distinguish the master from the apprentice, not mere knowledge. For this reason, practice, trial and error, as well as helping deliver value, were all a part of the apprentice model. It was an informal training and the apprentice grew in proportion to their desire to learn and their talents.

Examples of apprenticeship learning include Leonardo Di Vinci, Benjamin Franklin and Mark Twain.

Before the 2008 market crash, entry-level jobs were more abundant, but as the economy has shifted, fewer jobs returned even as the market recovered. There is a major shift happening in the economy; a shift from a crumbling Industrial Revolutionary market that Americans had enjoyed for nearly a century—a market where trainable, compliant workers once in demand saw those jobs shipped overseas— to a market that requires workers to be highly skilled in new areas, where being flexible, creative and a generalist are more important than compliance. The downturn has impacted the labor force in industries such as manufacturing and most middle management jobs.

Surely all of the "good jobs" would return to America when the economy recovered, but sadly, they did not, nor will they. The housing market crash revealed that the industrial model Americans had enjoyed has nearly vanished. The jobs that college grads were promised would be there wait-ing for them at the end of the college rainbow will be com-pletely transformed. The mantra: "Get good grades, go to a good college so you can get a good job," is becoming more and more scarce.

Why an apprenticeship, why a return to working for a master practitioner, learning new skills rather than applying the college major you earned? Remember, the result of be-ing an apprentice is that you learn you can create your own business and produce wealth for yourself, rather than report to a job.

The idea of showing up to a job is about a century old. Before the 1900s, people built value and shared their goods and services for money or other resources. The industrial machine didn't really accelerate until World War I when the demand for mass production kicked in full swing. Nowadays, we are not accustomed to making our own living; we have been persuaded that we must have a job, but we need to em-brace the shift back to individuals delivering value to others. I believe that we can create something great to serve the tribe we lead because of this revival of apprenticeship.

The good news is that it's never been easier to pick your-self and do something that matters. It has never been easier to get your gift to the world—you don't need permission to start something. Find an audience that cares and they will be grateful that you showed up and said, "Hey, I made something, check it out."

Chris Anderson, in his book *The Long Tail: Why The Future of Business is Selling Less of More*, describes that finding a small tribe of people that care about what you have to say is not merely possible, but it's revolutionizing our world. There are no longer just three TV networks that capture America's attention; there are thousands and thousands of ways into it and for sharing content—from YouTube to Netflix to Facebook. Everybody has a place to share in their gift in a world where connection is king. The question isn't whether I will share my gift; it is what *is* my gift.

Chris Guillebeau, in his book *The $100 Startup: Reinvent the Way You Make a Living, Do What You Love, and Create a New Future*, writes that you can't make a living out of every passion you have. For example, he argues that no one is going to pay you to eat pizza and play video games. It might be true that you won't be paid to do that, but if you love video games, there are tons of jobs that can relate to your passion that give you more time to do what you love.

People who start something based on their gift will be the ones who rule the future. They will be the ones to redesign the next chapter in the American Economy. If kids in dorm rooms can create companies such as Facebook, Dell Computers, Apple, etc., then what's keeping you from creating something? What we need is a society of learners that are willing to embrace the idea of taking the set of skills they have, discovering a passion, and then looking for the people that can help them build something great.

Chapter 10

Setting up Your Own Apprenticeship

"Be the change that you wish to see in the world."

—Mahatma Gandhi

In July 2014 President Obama's cabinet revised the call for more apprenticeship in America and his administration wants to create more skilled labor. This is great news because it will be much easier to tell people why you're creating your own apprenticeship. Companies such as Google, Facebook, and the like are now opting to develop their own young talent. I think in the future we'll see more companies create apprenticeships and begin to look for talented high school students rather college graduates to develop. These companies are looking for generalists who they can develop and have the skills to quickly adapt.

Here are some things to master as you prepare for your apprenticeship. You will want to have evidence that you are already on a path of learning before you reach out to a leader to create an apprenticeship. In the future I imagine there will be less of a need for resumes and more of a need for a way to show what you've done and how you can contribute to a company or organization.

Here are some practical ideas that you can apply when developing your own apprenticeship.

1. Create Something to Share. Before meeting a leader, be sure to have a way to share what you have been learning. If you have been doing some learning on your own, create a way to display it: a book, a blog, a photo book or some other tangible item. Don't show up with nothing to share. It will appear like you are not serious about learning. Use a professional photobook company, such as Shutterfly or Blurb, or if you don't want to create a physical book, maybe create a blog or social media page to feature what you are learning.

2. Plan to Have Some Setbacks. Be ready to bounce back quickly if the leader that you reach out to is not available to help at first. Chances are the top people in an industry are busy people. In order to practice bouncing back, set up some opportunities for rejection. Noah Keegan from AppSumo.

com, suggests creating a challenge to help you deal with rejection by going to a coffee shop such as Starbucks and order something and then ask for a 10% discount. Don't worry about what the outcome is, you are looking for the skill of handling rejection, not a discount, but it's an added bonus if it works!

3. Think and Act Like a Novice. Our attitudes about our own abilities cause us to try and hide our weaknesses. But to be someone's apprentice you will need to take a humble approach if you want to learn quickly. In order to overcome this, try taking classes about something new, something you have never attempted before and go through what it feels like to be a humble novice. Having this experience will mimic what it is like to create an effective apprenticeship. If you want to learn you must be prepared to feel a little dumb at first.

4. Be Childish. *Play is good, so find ways to play.* Maybe play a card game like Go Fish or organize an adult version of hide and seek. If you feel a bit silly, that is the point—play is a sign of a child-like heart and you can learn a lot from someone while playing. Be uncomfortable join a kickball league or go sing karaoke or just put the radio on and have a dance party—just play. Don't run from the uncomfortable feeling of play—embrace it.

5. Practice Making Cold Calls. One thing I learned from my friends at the organization Roadtrip Nation is how important it is to have the skill of making a cold-call. Roadtrip Nation empowers individuals to explore who they are and what they want to do with their lives. One of the founders, Brian McAllister, and his co-founders graduated college and still didn't know what they wanted to do with their adult lives so they took an RV and traveled the country asking leaders they admired how they got to where they are. Through their travels they were able to interview a Supreme Court Justice; the CEO of Starbucks, Howard Schultz; and Dell CEO, Michael Dell. They were able to land all of these interviews because they made cold-calls. I want you to do the same task that Roadtrip Nation asks its students to do, call a restaurant and ask them how to make a baked potato. I know that it seems crazy but just tell them you are doing some preparation for an apprenticeship. Don't change the task just do it. Making cold calls is essential.

6. Create a Mind Map. Creating a mind map is a way of designing a learning contract, a feasible plan with dates and times when you are going to get things done. For example, say your plan is to create a new relationship with a leader. When do you plan to speak with him? When will you send the email? By what date will you meet the person? Will it be online? A Google chat or a Skype call? For example, I want to start a podcast but have no experience so I have to create a mind map about what I already know and what I will need to get a highly successful podcast started. A mind map is sort of like a web that you did in middle school when asked to brainstorm a story—the main topic in the middle and all of the things you know or need to know around the edges.

7. Reach Out To a Leader. *The most important thing is to reach out.* It will feel a bit intimidating either making a call or sending an email to someone you admire, but it's necessary. Don't avoiding making the call or sending an email. It will just prevent you from moving forward. It's important to make sure the leader you choose is somebody you really want to meet. You may be a bit nervous and that's how you know it's the right person. The worst that can happen is they say no or don't respond.

8. Conduct an Informal Interview. When you meet your leader be sure to touch base and have a clear sense of how much time they have. You don't want to start off the relationship with the idea that you will be taking tons of time from their schedule. Write down some simple but meaningful open-ended questions before the interview, be prepared, but also know it's not a magazine interview—it's informal. Start by asking about how they arrived where they are and to tell a bit about their story. If time allows, be sure to tell them that you are on a learning journey. Listen more than talk and if there is time at the end of the conversation ask if they have one piece of advice for you. If things seem to go well, ask if you can reach out to them again if you have some more questions. Perhaps from this you can form a relationship that can lead to building a meaningful apprenticeship. Do not force it, but be sure to ask how you might follow up with what you are learning. Don't give up if the first person you talk to is not a match—think of it as practice for the next interview.

9. Take Their Advice. If the person you interview suggests that you do something, be sure to act on what they say. It's a great way to follow up if you say that you are reconnecting about the outcomes or discoveries you made by following their advice. Ask if you could meet again sometime to discuss what you learned. This is a good time to show off your book or website or actionable item. If they are busy, send a hand-written note thanking them for the advice. Either way, it will be a step forward because you will be acting upon their recommendations.

10. Ask About Creating an Apprenticeship. Most people are new to the idea of an apprenticeship. They are more likely familiar with the idea of an internship. Most likely they will have in their mind if you want an "internship" you must be in school. They might even think that an apprenticeship can only be arranged if you are in school, but the law is pretty clear what governs an "internship-like" relationship. If you are lucky a mentor won't mind showing you a few things

97

if you make this an informal arrangement. If they're not willing to give you an apprenticeship, maybe at least they'll give you a tour of the place where they work or share some of their work habits or secrets about how to get work done. If they agree to the apprenticeship, be sure to follow The Department of Labor's clear guidelines about Internship Programs under The Fair Labor Standards Act.

11. Establish Clear Expectations. If they agree to have you as an apprentice, set up clear guidelines and expectations. Lay out what you would like to get out of the experience as well as what you have to offer. It might be a good idea to have a clear amount of time for the apprenticeship— maybe you will work evenings, or take two weeks of your vacation from an existing job, or work on weekends in your spare time. Remember an apprenticeship is an informal or tacit way of learning.

12. Focus on the Most Important Learning. If you're serious about becoming a master practitioner and getting the most out of your apprenticeship, remember the 80/20 rule: focus on the 20% of the learning that gives you 80% of the success. For example, in order to write this book I needed to imitate best-selling authors, so I joined the Bestselling Book System with Chandler Bolt, James Roper, and Tyler

Wagner because each one had made it to best seller status on Amazon. I focused the 20% of what I needed to do to get this book done and to best seller status. I didn't worry about the small things that could have taken all of my time such as grammar, over editing, or creating the perfect book. I spent my time getting the book written and marketed, which is what made the launch so successful. My goal was to be a best-selling, published author, not to be the best author.

13. Make Your Goals Public. Let people know you're up to something. Tell your inner circles that you are learning something new, that you are trying to reach out to leaders and that you want to connect. Remember, avoid the vampires and zombies but do find ways to share what you are up to. Post your goals on social media. Tell people at parties or those you meet that you are excited that you are following your passion, and tell them you have a plan to start something new. Tell them when you plan to do this.

14. Give, Give, Give. Be grateful—remember, we started this journey with gratitude. Don't lose that focus. Remember the offer to help other people that supported you during your journey. Remember your gift is to be shared with the world.

Building an apprenticeship is like constructing a path to a new life—one that is full of passion and joy. If you have wanted to make a change in your life, to find a new career, or have work that fills your soul, then it's time to take action.

ABOUT THE AUTHOR

Azul is a national and international leader in educational entrepreneurship; project based learning and innovative learning practices. His undergraduate and graduate education at UCLA helped prepare him to serve as a coach to schools and organizations worldwide including the USA, Australia, Canada, China, India, Israel, Spain and Chile.

A month before Azul enrolled in the 1 Day Business Breakthrough hosted by Chris Ducker and Pat Flynn, he didn't yet have a business and he'd only dreamed of becoming an entrepreneur. Azul challenged himself to write and complete the manuscript for this book in 30 days in order to have something to talk about when he landed in the hotseat. His lifelong love of learning and passion to help others to pursue their dreams led him to become a writing coach. He went on to self-publish this book and become a bestseller on Amazon within three months. Now he coaches writers around the world and has developed a successful business helping others tell their stories.

When he is not writing or teaching he is participating in Slam Storytelling, connecting with like-minded entrepreneurs and traveling the world with his partner and two teenage children. He currently lives in Shanghai, China where he spends his time building a community of individuals dedicated to igniting their passions and making a living doing what they love.

Thank You For Reading My Book! Scooter and I appreciate all of your feedback and I would love to hear from you and what you have to say about the book.

Please leave your honest review on Amazon.com

I'd love to hear from you!

I'm on Facebook at azul.terronez or find me on Twitter @AzulTerronez

You are a rock star!

—Azul